PORTRAITS

Canadian Women in Focus

PORTRAITS

Canadian Women in Focus

BARBARA WOODLEY
foreword by Peter Gzowski

Barbara Woodley
'92

DOUBLEDAY CANADA LIMITED

FINNING
FINNING LIMITED

LABATT BREWERIES OF CANADA

MAINSTREAM ACCESS CORPORATION

▲Hemlock
The performance printers
HEMLOCK PRINTERS

CANADIAN CATALOGUING IN PUBLICATION DATA

Woodley, Barbara

    Portraits: Canadian women in focus

ISBN 0-385-25309-5

1. Women – Canada – Portraits. 2. Canada – Biography – Portraits 1. Title

FC25.W6 1992   779'.24'0971   C91-095487-9

F1005.W6 1992

All photographs were printed by Barbara Woodley using Kodak Elite Fine Art Paper

Editorial, production and design supervision: Maggie Reeves

Design by Tania Craan

Typesetting by Colborne, Cox & Burns Inc.

Printed and bound in Canada by Hemlock Printers

Published in Canada by

Doubleday Canada Limited

105 Bond Street

Toronto, Ontario

M5B 1Y3

For my Mom, Linda

Contents

Foreword **ix**

Photographer's Note **xii**

Acknowledgements **xiv**

1   Hon. Barbara McDougall
2   Muriel Duckworth
3   Lisa Borsholt-Greenwood
4   Kimiko Okano Murakami
5   June Callwood
6   Anne Wheeler
7   Dr. Lois Wilson
8   Gathie Falk
9   Dulcie McCallum
10   Mary Pratt
11   Susan Musgrave
12   Liona Boyd
13   Sister Mary Greene
14   Gladys Angley
15   Susan Nattrass
16   Dr. Julia Levy
17   Maureen Forrester
18   Dinah Christie
19   Alice Kane
20   Hon. Beverley McLachlin
21   Helen Sawyer Hogg
22   Margo Timmins
23   P.K. Page
24   Marion Quednau
25   Rosemary Brown
26   Nancy Greene Raine
27   Rosella Bjornson
28   Rt. Hon. Jeanne Sauvé
29   Louise Ardenne
30   Brenda and Charlene Taylor
31   Doris Anderson
32   Dr. Mary-Wynne Ashford
33   Doris Shadbolt

34   Claudia Kerckhoff-Van Wijk
35   Daphne Odjig
36   Anne Cameron
37   Col. the Hon. Pauline McGibbon
38   Vicki Keith
39   Hon. Sylvia Fedoruk
40   Buffy Sainte-Marie
41   Dorothy Livesay
42   Marjorie Blackhurst
43   Carolyn Waldo-Baltzer
44   Dr. Geraldine Kenney-Wallace
45   Dr. Margaret Somerville
46   Dr. Glenda Simms
47   May Gutteridge
48   Leila Joy MacKenzie
49   Edith Fowke
50   Janet Parsons
51   Evelyn Hart
52   Jean Coulthard
53   Phyllis Lambert
54   Jean Little
55   Joni Mitchell
56   Alice Munro
57   Juliette
58   Hon. Claire L'Heureux-Dubé
59   Cynthia Dale
60   Adrienne Clarkson
61   Jane Rule
62   Mary Masales
63   Debbie Brill
64   Hon. Kim Campbell
65   Rita MacNeil
66   Sharon Wood

Foreword

The most memorable dinner party of my life took place in the summer of 1990, and since it not only played some small part in the history of this quite remarkable book but serves as a symbol of some of the reasons I think it — the book — *is* remarkable, I beg the reader's indulgence if I dwell on it for a moment before turning you over to the real contents herein.

The occasion was my birthday (my fifty-sixth, if that matters); the main dish was roast lamb, and the guests, nine of them — there are seven in the pages that lie ahead — were some of the most compelling women in this country. I was the only male.

The party had had its genesis about a year earlier. When my boss at the time, Gloria Bishop, had turned fifty, she had decided to indulge herself with a dinner at which she'd be the only *woman*. She'd drawn up a list, talked a friend into helping with the invitations and the cooking (and then disappearing), and, on the night itself, found herself surrounded by six of us in dinner jackets, toasting her health and generally making a fuss over her. I had a wonderful time — I think we all did, including Gloria — and, some time later I began wondering what it would be like to turn, as it were, the tables. A fantasy. Still, never one to waste an idea, I decided to write about it in *Canadian Living* magazine, where I do a monthly column.

Making my guest-list turned out to be both the most pleasant and the most difficult part of my reverie. The pleasure lay in going through the memories of some of the hundreds and hundreds of interviews I've been lucky enough to have with women over the years I've worked in print, radio and television. The difficulty, of course, was in trying to winnow that catalogue down to a manageable number, small enough to fit into both my dining room and the single page I'm afforded at *Canadian Living*, but large enough, this being Canada, not to be confined to a single geographical region. In the end, I chose ten women I thought would not only make good company for me but would enjoy each other — that part, at least, being precisely like composing a real party. I wrote my column, smiling as I imagined what the conversation would be like, sent it to my editors, and forgot about it.

I had not reckoned with the sort of guests I'd chosen. At least one of them — I'm pretty sure the instigator was Dulcie McCallum, whose blithe spirit you can see peering out from Photo #9 here — decided the idea was too good to exist only in my imagination. Without the slightest hint to me, they began calling each other around the country, checking their date books, counting their air-travel points, scheming. On my birthday, to my astonishment, they conspired with both the woman I live with and my children to lure me away from my country retreat and into downtown Toronto. There they were, nine of my ten friends, from as far away as Yellowknife, the only absentee being the ballerina Evelyn Hart, who was dancing in Munich at the time and sent, in her place, a poster of the Royal Winnipeg Ballet's *Romeo and Juliet*, my hirsute mug pasted over the visage of her partner.

Barbara McDougall was there, sporting a straw hat as big as a wagon wheel and Dinah Christie, full of gossip from her latest adventures in television. As a birthday present, Debbie Brill brought a print she had made of the outline of her own trim rear end — a rear end, I realized as I joined in the delighted laughter at the table, that had soared to some record heights in its day — and Mary-Wynne Ashford, the doctor and peace activist, brought a survival kit of homemade jams, poetry, and wisdom. Margaret Somerville, Margo to her friends, whom I'd described in my column as the smartest woman in Canada, sat at my left and Alice Munro, the greatest short-story writer in the English language was at the . . . Well, enough.

The connection with this book? Small, as I say, but real. Barbara Woodley, as I was to learn much later, was in full pursuit of her quarry when the article about my dinner party appeared in *Canadian Living*, and, as she was doing with so many other sources, she found some suggested subjects among my guests. (As I also learned later, she was listening to *Morningside* most mornings, too, her ear cocked for ideas.)

The other link? In a word, it's celebration. Self-indulgence aside, the real reason I wanted to construct my imaginary guest list in a national magazine was to give my readers some idea of the incredible number of gifted, able, accomplished, *fascinating* women in their midst. On one page, I could scarcely begin. Here, in 152 pages, Barbara Woodley has come much closer. And just as she was able to find some ideas for subjects of her camera in my work, so do I, making my happy way among these marvellous photographs, find myself discovering new possible interviews.

Or, for that matter, future guests for a fantasy dinner.

One more thought if I may.

There is a very special vision in these pages; a unique, playful, quirky, powerful point of view. Though I have met — albeit often for not much more than my usual fifteen minutes — some fifty of the sixty-six women who appear here, there is not one with whom I do not instantly see something in Barbara Woodley's photograph I have not seen before, from Kim Campbell's tongue-in-cheek earthiness to the serenity of June Callwood. I see both the femininity of their power and the power of their femininity. I both know all these women better for having seen them here and want to know them more. How Barb Woodley — as she signs her occasional, pixie-ish notes to me — has accomplished that, I haven't the faintest idea. But I know we are lucky to have her among us; a new voice with a camera, a new and intriguing recorder of our times.

Peter Gzowski

Photographer's Note

The idea for this collection began in the spring of 1989. I went with friends to hear Canadian mountaineer Sharon Wood speak of her climb to the summit of Mount Everest.

After hearing her story, I was moved. To climb Mount Everest is truly an amazing feat. What I found to be equally amazing though, was that I, and many others, were completely unaware that the first North American woman to reach the summit of the highest mountain in the world was a Canadian.

The apparent lack of pride we show for Canadians who have accomplished wonderful things with their lives sometimes frustrates me. I have always felt that acknowledging the contributions people have made encourages others to look beyond their limitations and see the possibilities within themselves.

Subconsciously, Sharon's story must have encouraged me for the next morning, at about three o'clock, I awoke from a dream. I dreamt I had travelled across Canada seeking out and photographing inspirational Canadians: people who were accomplished in the arts, business, humanitarianism, and sports; people who had achieved firsts. People like Sharon Wood. I wrote a letter to the women I wished to photograph, and with help from Finning Limited, I packed up my vehicle and drove across the country. The dream became a reality.

And so the collection began.

Meeting and photographing these women was indeed inspirational. In their presence you immediately become aware of their gift. Both their strength and spirit are instantly obvious. They are dedicated to their talents and their work, each one connected by a thread common to all.

Surprisingly, as I travelled across Canada documenting more and more of these inspirational women, I realized that my frustration was not shared by the subjects of this book. Jane Rule (photo #61) reflects upon this phenomenon when she says, "The artist in Canada must still be willing to make great sacrifices without the promise of conventional success. The only sure reward is the love of the work." This quote explains so much. These women do what they do, not for reward or recognition, but because they must. It is this innate characteristic that is their shared thread — a gift that left me genuinely inspired after meeting every one of them.

I was grateful for the trust some had in me during the photo sessions. I was allowed to photograph them as I viewed them, not as they would necessarily view themselves. I am certain my ideas for Sharon Wood, Margo Timmins, and Mary Pratt, to name but a few, were somewhat awkward for them. Yet I believe they could only collaborate with me because of their own self-assuredness seasoned with a wonderful sense of humour.

From the moment I began this book I knew I wanted journalist Peter Gzowski to introduce the work. I learned more about Canadians through Peter than any other source. I admire his respect for these people and his own methods of documenting. He seems to feel what I feel and says what I want to say. And when I begin my collection of photographs of Canadian men, I shall begin with him.

For now, however, I shall continue to build this collection, as this book is only a small representation of our inspirational Canadian women. Included here are women from Victoria, British Columbia to St. Marys, Newfoundland and yet the Nellie Cournyeas, Margaret Atwoods, and Wendy Dobsons are absent. Undoubtedly, as you view the pages to come, you will think of additional inspirations, both new and old, who should be acknowledged. To document all of Canada's inspirations would indeed be a life-long mission.

My sincere thanks to the women in this book for allowing me, and those inspired by you, the honour of your portrait.

Barbara Woodley

Acknowledgements

This project owes its existence to Finning Limited, one of the world's largest equipment dealers, based in Vancouver, British Columbia. An international company with operations in Western Canada and Europe, Finning was the sole sponsor during the first eighteen months of production. Its continuous support of this project demonstrates Finning's commitment to the arts and the athletic, environmental, and social endeavours in all the communities that Finning serves. My special thanks goes to Vincent Coyne, Finning's manager of corporate communications, for his vision, advice, and encouragement about *Portraits*.

The support of Labatt Breweries of Canada has given *Portraits* a completely new dimension. Labatt is the largest Canadian-owned brewer and one of the largest brewers in the world. Traditionally, Labatt is a major supporter of Canadian artists and I appreciated the company's decision to organize and sponsor a cross-country tour of the photographic collection. People in major centres across Canada will now have an opportunity to see *Portraits* and become aware of the achievements of a remarkable group of Canadian women. Labatt's participation helped make this book a reality and I would like to express my sincere thanks to Tim Vauthier, executive vice-president of human resources, and Sharon Paul, executive vice-president of public affairs.

I would also like to thank J.A. Warner Woodley, president and chief executive officer of Mainstream Access Corporation, who had the insight to promote *Portraits* in a first-class fashion and who gave this project exposure by exhibiting the photographs in his company's offices across Canada. Mainstream Access is a national career and organizational renewal consulting firm that is dedicated to assisting individuals and organizations make successful transitions. Mainstream's commitment to making a difference is clearly reflected in the work of the artist and in the outstanding achievement of the Canadian women portrayed.

The Canada Council Explorations Program awarded the project a grant in August 1990. My sincere appreciation to Richard Holden for his genuine encouragement and to the jurors for their consideration and much needed support.

My thanks to the women in this book for their direct contribution to the text. The first person material came from several different sources, but in most cases it was in response to a questionnaire sent out by my publisher. The resulting text complements the photographs and helps to form a true portrait of each woman. The text was gathered and edited by Jill Lambert, associate editor at Doubleday Canada, and I would like to thank her for this, and for her perseverance in general.

I would like to thank the print production team for the quality of this book. The experience of Doubleday Publishing Manager Maggie Reeves, the generosity of Hemlock President Dick Kouwenhoven, the professionalism of Account Executive Paul Lamb and the abilities of Technical Director Barrie Heyes and his team at Hemlock Printers have made a great contribution to this project.

All subjects were photographed with Kodak's TMAX-100 film and exhibition prints were printed on Kodak Elite Fine Art Paper. My sincere thanks to Professional Imaging, Kodak Canada and especially to Lauragaye Jackson and Holly Nightingale for putting this project into Kodak's lecture series 1992 program. This program gave me the opportunity to travel across Canada from Victoria, B.C. to Charlottetown, P.E.I., speaking about these inspirational Canadians.

My grateful thanks to Harry Franklin Jr., whose support will always be appreciated, to Elly Den Outsden, Rosemary Birney, Geoffrey Bird, Dr. Turner and Sarah Verchère, Halina and Ken Nicholson, Gregg Wiltshire, Lynn Chase, Jennifer Crocker, Roberta Kent, Murray Price, Howard Shaw Productions, Showmakers', and First Pass Imaging, who all played special roles, and to my teachers Gerry Blitstein and Bill Lewis. Thanks to all those people I met while driving across Canada who gave me ideas of inspirational Canadians, who lent me props, walls, and backyards in which to photograph these women.

Also, my gratitude to the managers, assistants, and representatives of these Canadian women who received my letter in the mail and decided it should be forwarded to the hands of the people you have viewed in this book.

And most of all, thank you to my parents Glenn and Linda Woodley, my brother David, and my sisters Deborah and Glenda. During the eighteen months it took to photograph and print these portraits, they were my inspiration, my assistants, my strongest critics, and my best friends. I love you.

PORTRAITS

Canadian Women in Focus

The Honourable
Barbara McDougall

Secretary of State for External Affairs

"If I had to pick out the things that have supported me throughout my political career, it would be the same things that have carried me through my life. First, my family who have been my touchstone and reality-check in this different and difficult world of politics. Second, the network of friends I have developed who have an infinite variety of points of view and who have taught me to respect the opinions of others as well as a politician's greatest skill — the capacity to listen."

Barbara McDougall's rise to power has been fast and highly visible. She started her career as an investment analyst, eventually becoming a vice-president of Dominion Securities Ames Ltd. By 1982, she was executive director of the Canadian Council of Financial Analysts, a position she held until 1984, when she was elected to Parliament to represent the Toronto riding of St. Paul's. She has been responsible for several portfolios in the cabinet, including Status of Women and Employment and Immigration. She currently holds one of the most critical positions in the cabinet as the Secretary of State for External Affairs.

Muriel Duckworth

Activist, Civil Libertarian, and Peace Worker

"It seems to me that there are two layers of people in the world: the powerful ones in politics, industry, and the military; and the masses of people in poverty, ignorance, and oppression. People like me have to decide whose side we are on and make it known, by our actions, where we stand. Getting into the action is essential for the defence of all human rights — for those of women, children, aboriginal peoples, prisoners, refugees, and homosexuals."

Muriel Duckworth has spent over fifty years working to ensure women's rights and to bring about a non-violent society. She was a founding member and president of Voice of Women, Canada and later president of the Canadian Research Institute for the Advancement of Women. She is a founding member of fourteen citizens' associations and for her work she has received six honorary degrees and many awards, including the Order of Canada and the Pearson Peace Medal. She has worked for Oxfam and UNICEF Canada, and she is on the advisory boards of the Peace Fund of Canada, the World Federalists of Canada, and *Atlantis: A Women's Study Journal*. She has held all of these positions as a volunteer.

Lisa Borsholt-Greenwood

Swimmer

"It is important to set goals for oneself, challenging yet attainable, and focus and dedicate oneself towards reaching those goals. Recognize who you are and what you are capable of and continue to strive — in all aspects of your life — and in the end you will be the best person you can be."

Lisa Borsholt-Greenwood first got her feet wet in the world of competitive swimming when she joined a swim club at the age of thirteen. She eventually became a member of the Canadian National Swim Team, taking home a gold medal from the 1978 Commonwealth Games in Edmonton, Alberta. At the Olympic trials in 1984 she won gold again, this time for the 100-metre breaststroke. Lisa Borsholt-Greenwood's swimming career spanned three Olympic Games.

Kimiko Okano Murakami

Japanese-Canadian Pioneer

"Challenges have been the catalyst of her resolve to succeed in goals that she constantly set for herself and her family. We children reflect upon her efforts as the ultimate sacrifice for our survival and achievements. She sees these sacrifices as merely tasks that she chose to do. In her conversations, there is never a hint of her sufferings or the sacrifices she made for the family's survival. Instead, when in her presence one feels the aura of strength that enabled her to succeed in life."

To have lost everything she owned and cherished, to have been imprisoned for eight years, to have the land she loved taken from her, and then to return and not be bitter. That is Kimiko Okano Murakami, who remains an inspiration to her children and all who know her. She was the first Japanese baby born in Steveston, British Columbia in 1904. In 1942, despite her Canadian background, her husband was taken away, his fate unknown to her, and the family suffered the indignities of incarceration and the eventual loss of their seventeen acres on Salt Spring Island. Reunited, the family eventually returned to the island with both good memories and bad. Focused on the important things in life, Kimiko Okano Murakami inspires her six children to move only forward, to a future of happiness and achievement. Her daughter speaks for her:

June Callwood

Journalist and Civil Libertarian

"I love journalism, a profession with a long history in Canada of carrying the spirit of reform like a banner at the head of a parade. A free-lance journalist, as I have been for over fifty years, has the opportunity to listen to many voices, to hang out in archives, to check out the front lines where today's need collides with yesterday's response, and to aspire to be an eloquent witness so that attitudinal change can occur. Journalists who can't or won't be silenced are indispensible to the growth of democracy."

June Callwood is known for her literary triumphs as well as her tireless devotion to human rights. She has written twenty-four books, including *Love, Hate, Fear, Anger, and Other Lively Emotions, The Law is Not for Women, Portrait of Canada, Twelve Weeks in Spring, Jim: A Life with AIDS,* and *The Sleepwalker*. She was until 1989 a columnist for *The Globe and Mail* and during her career she has contributed over four hundred articles to national magazines such as *Maclean's* and *Chatelaine*. June Callwood was the founder of Jessie's Centre for Teenagers, Nellie's Hostel for Women, Casey House Hospice, and a founding member of both ACTRA and The Writer's Union of Canada. She has received eleven honorary doctorates, the Order of Canada twice, and the Order of Ontario.

Anne Wheeler

Film Maker

"I am a storyteller, plain and simple, not unlike the storytellers of old. My stories permit people to see themselves and those they know well. This can be entertaining, but it may also reveal some understanding that will be useful in their own lives. I try not to be moralistic, and I always hope that everyone who watches one of my films will see something unique within themselves."

Anne Wheeler is an award-winning film maker who has directed, written, and/or produced dozens of films since the early 1970s. Her career began with small productions — her first project was three commercials on how to brush your teeth — and each one since has been a little larger and a little more ambitious. Her early work was primarily documentary, while her later work is dramatic. She is now well known for her feature films such as *Cowboys Don't Cry* and *Bye Bye Blues*. Her films are often about her prairie homeland, and tell stories of ordinary people caught up in extraordinary circumstances.

Dr. Lois Wilson

Minister

"To be authentically human is to centre one's life on the world God loves. That beloved world is sick unto death and needs caretakers, lovers, gardeners, and partners who commit themselves to preserving life rather than dealing death. I try to be such a person."

Lois Wilson, currently chancellor of Lakehead University, is a former president of the World Council of Churches, former moderator of the United Church of Canada, and former president of the Canadian Council of Churches. Ordained a minister in 1965, she shared team ministry in various Ontario cities with her husband Roy for fifteen years. Her work focuses on human rights, peace, ecumenicism, feminism, and the significance of faith communities in a global context. She has been awarded eleven honorary degrees from Canadian universities, the Order of Canada, the Order of Ontario, and the Canadian United Nations Pearson Peace Prize. She is the author of two books, her most recent being *Turning the World Upside Down*.

Gathie Falk

Artist

"Canada is a good place in which to work. One is not going to be seized by the scruff of the neck after one's first few scribblings and hurled into a position of fame and fortune. One is not made to repeat endlessly what one has done before in order to hold a favoured position. One is rolled back and forth gently; never too much fame, never totally ignored when one has put out a sufficiently large body of work. It's a condition to keep the head cool, the brush warm, the footsteps to the studio hopeful, the heart grateful for small compliments."

Gathie Falk is a painter, a sculptor, and a performance artist who has established her reputation in scores of exhibitions across Canada and elsewhere. Her many accomplishments include her commissioned work, "Diary" for the Canadian Embassy in Washington, D.C. Major art galleries from Victoria to Halifax, including the National Gallery of Canada, have her work as a part of their permanent collections. She is the recipient of five Canada Council Awards and was honoured with the Sun Award in 1968 and the Gershon Iskowitz Prize in 1990.

Dulcie McCallum

Lawyer and Ombudsman

"What I have learned from knowing people with intellectual impairments, as friends and as co-workers, has changed my life. I see my role as facilitator, enabling people previously excluded and discredited to speak for themselves, encouraging others to listen. I am but one of many Canadians who for the first time in history are speaking a new language and understanding a new way of thinking that will mean the successful and meaningful inclusion of all Canadians regardless of disability."

"A mature Anne of Green Gables who breathes fire" best describes Dulcie McCallum. The quote comes from Jack Batten, author of *On Trial*, a book about one of a series of legal challenges across the country aimed at ensuring that all children, regardless of disability, have the opportunity to be included in their neighbourhood school alongside their friends and family. Dulcie McCallum is currently a lawyer and government affairs consultant for the Canadian Association for Community Living, which advocates with and on behalf of all people who have a mental handicap. She began her career as a registered nurse — working in hospitals, prisons, and finally as a community health nurse for the Haida Indians. She was called to the Bar of British Columbia in 1983. In 1992 Dulcie McCallum was appointed British Columbia's first female ombudsman. She has one daughter, Juel Charlotte.

Mary Pratt

Artist

"The great advantage of being a woman is that one can develop unobserved. Parents still have higher hopes and bigger plans for sons than they do for daughters. As a result, girls can often choose their own paths. I was one of those lucky girls who has had the great fortune to do what I passionately love to do — paint. If all the people who see my paintings could realize even a little of the passion I feel when I paint them — I'd be very happy."

When Mary Pratt was ten years old, she had a painting accepted for an international children's exhibition at the Luxembourg Museum in Paris. When she was forty years old, she had a group of paintings shown at the National Gallery of Canada as part of the gallery's tribute to Canadian women artists. These are two highlights of her career but in between she has had many shows across Canada and internationally. She is on the Canada Council and has been on many boards and committees dealing with the arts, fisheries, education, international trade and the legal profession. In 1989, a book entitled *Mary Pratt* was published to celebrate the work of this outstanding Canadian artist.

Susan Musgrave

Writer

"It's been ages since I crossed out any days on my calendar. While death may be inevitable, I have learned to set shorter-term goals for myself in the meantime. I go on because my daughter has her tap-dancing lesson after school, I have a pre-natal class later in the week, and my husband needs to know what colour to paint the drywall over the weekend."

Susan Musgrave left high school in Grade 10. Everybody told her she was going too far, but she believed that far was the only place worth going. Her first poems were published in *The Malahat Review* when she was sixteen. Her first collection of poetry, *Songs of the Sea-Witch*, was published to wide acclaim when she was only nineteen. She has gone on to publish nine more books of poetry, three children's books, two novels, and a non-fiction book about the writer's life called *Great Musgrave*. In 1986 she married Stephen Reid, author of *Jackrabbit Parole*, while he was in a maximum security prison serving a twenty-year sentence for gold robbery.

Liona Boyd

Guitarist

Liona Boyd is an internationally renowned classical guitarist, who has performed both solo and orchestral concerts in dozens of countries throughout the world and has brought classical music to wide audiences through her many concerts and recordings. Several of her seventeen albums have gone gold and platinum. She has been awarded the Order of Canada, the Vanier Award, three honorary doctorates, and four Juno awards. Canada's "First Lady of the Guitar" has played Summit conferences and Royal Command Performances. In recent years she has turned her hand to composing and includes original pieces in her repertoire.

"I have always felt that music contributes profoundly to the richness and beauty of life. I have been fortunate to be able to share my talent on the classical guitar with people all over the world, transcending the barriers of language, culture, and politics.

It was in Canada, however, that my studies and career first began and I'm very grateful to the Canadian people for the love and continued appreciation they have shown me over the years."

Sister Mary Greene

Humanitarian

Mary Greene was born on the Gaspé coast and received her teaching certificate in 1922 at age seventeen. She joined a group of lay teachers and together they built a new congregation in Campbellton, New Brunswick. Mary Greene was soon appointed to the administrative board and has since devoted her life to helping the poor of Campbellton — a never-ending task. She has been given many awards for her work, including an honorary Ph.D. in social work from the University of Moncton. She was made a member of the Order of Canada in 1981.

"Feminism and feminists were words seldom heard in 1922, and yet I firmly believe that the valiant women working with me unobtrusively, unceasingly, and determinedly, were, in their own way, feminists. We paved the way for the future generations of women who pick up the flame and with equal generosity and determination, but with much more effective means, strive to make the world a better place. To these I say: don't quit, persevere in your demands, reach out with both hands, a reassuring one to our abused sisters, the other, persuasive, to those whose duty it is to second your efforts and implant just laws."

13 – September 29, 1989   Campbellton, New Brunswick

Gladys Angley

Piano Instructor

"Yesterday I said to one of my students, 'I get my spirit from all you little pupils' and the student responded, 'But oh Miss Angley, you give it to us.' I thought that was very sweet and generous. All the students are very loving and I feel I live in an atmosphere of love and I'm very blessed in that direction."

A lesson with Gladys Angley was more than a lesson at the piano, it was a lesson in life. The piano was simply an instrument by which she could also teach positive thinking and self-esteem. She earned a degree from the Toronto Conservatory and the Royal School of Music in London, England in the early 1930s. From 1941 to her retirement in 1980, she taught at the University of Regina's music department. Former students often returned for her wisdom on matters unrelated to the keys. Even a crippling disease couldn't keep Gladys Angley away from teaching; fragile from arthritis for many years, she continued to teach up to twenty-two students per week until she passed away at age seventy-eight, just two months after this portrait was taken.

Susan Nattrass

Trapshooter

"You always represent your country when it says Canada across your back. You just get used to it. I'm very proud of my country. I think it's fabulous and the more I travel the world the more I realize what a good thing we've got. But I don't let it be a burden on me that it says Canada on my back. I think I'm a good representative of my country. And I think it's important to be a good representative of yourself too."

Susan Nattrass was the first woman to compete in the Olympic trapshooting event in Olympic history. She was a gold medalist and world record holder in numerous international events, including world trapshooting championships in Switzerland, Germany, France, Korea, Italy, and Argentina. She was inducted into the Canadian Sports Hall of Fame and, in 1981, was named the Top Canadian Athlete of the year and an Officer of the Order of Canada.

Dr. Julia Levy

Scientist

"I always knew I wanted to do something. That something became some aspect of biology after I went to university. The wonder I felt when I first learned of the complexity of the workings of living cells made my first decision clear for me. Choosing medical research came from my interest in the basic questions that needed to be asked and my desire to do something useful in my life."

Julia Levy is the vice-president of discovery for Quadra Logic Technologies and industrial professor of microbiology at the University of British Columbia. Her work in immunology and tumour biology has been instrumental in the development of a promising new cancer treatment called Photodynamic Therapy. She is a Fellow of the Royal Society of Canada, and a recipient of both the Gold Medal from the Science Council of British Columbia and the Killam University Research Award. In 1987, she was appointed to the National Advisory Board on Science and Technology by Prime Minister Brian Mulroney.

Maureen Forrester

Opera Singer

"You can be anything you want to be if you have the energy. People say 'if only' but you have to do it for yourself. I started my career in Canada and chose to do the little things, to gain experience, and to let my career build so that by the time I was ready to face New York, for example, I had something to stand on. It's important to be a confident person on the inside."

Maureen Forrester's beautiful contralto voice has brought joy to audiences around the world. But it's not just her singing that brings her fame — she has also been the chairperson of the Canada Council and she is an active spokesperson for The Arthritis Society. Her career as an opera and concert singer was built up slowly, nurtured in the church choirs and ladies' clubs of Montreal in the 1950s. She is a strong believer in will power, which isn't surprising in someone with only six months of high school and twenty-nine honorary degrees.

Dinah Christie

Singer and Comedienne

"One creates. In the back of one's mind the hope lingers that the creation will touch another's heart, perhaps please them and, conceivably, contribute to their day . . . or even, life. It's the creation, itself, that is the end."

Peter Gzowski once wrote "In a country that knew better how to treat its stars, Dinah Christie would be up somewhere around Carol Channing." She has performed with Bob Hope, George Burns, and Don Adams and toured all over the world with *Tom Kneebone, in Concert*. Dinah lives on a small farm in southern Ontario and continues to sing and dance for fundraising causes.

Alice Kane

Storyteller

"I love mystery and fairy tales and the great wonder tales that go on through the ages and over the world unchanged. I like to be a link in the chain."

Alice Kane was born in the north of Ireland just before World War I. Her father was a sailor and only came home at six-week intervals, until, in 1921, the family followed him to a shore job in New Brunswick. Alice was a shy child, buried in books and frightened at the thought of playing a grown-up part in the busy world. It wasn't until she began her career as a children's librarian that she discovered the release of storytelling. After forty-three years as a children's librarian she retired to become a storyteller. She has told stories at schools, universities, festivals, and other gatherings in Great Britain, New York, Tennessee, and across Canada. She was a founder of the Storytellers School of Toronto and she is also the author of *Songs and Sayings of an Ulster Childhood*.

The Honourable Madame Justice Beverley McLachlin

Supreme Court Judge

"I chose the law because it promised to combine intellectual challenge with the opportunity to work with people. I have not been disappointed. I consider myself fortunate to have been able to pursue my legal career in this country, which increasingly recognizes the importance of women in its legal institutions. I would like to be remembered as a judge who cared about the law and about people."

Beverley McLachlin was born in Pincher Creek, Alberta. She tenured as a professor at the University of British Columbia. In 1981, she was appointed as a judge to the County Court of Vancouver and later the same year, to the Supreme Court of British Columbia. In 1985, she was appointed to the Court of Appeal of British Columbia; in 1988, as the Chief Justice of the Supreme Court of British Columbia; and, in 1989, to the Supreme Court of Canada.

Helen Sawyer Hogg

Astronomer

"I have led a reasonably balanced life — I am not an ivory tower scientist. My husband and I were a fine team and paid much attention to our three children, who never came home from school to an empty house. I taught at university level and wrote a weekly newspaper column for thirty years, but I managed to help with my seven grandchildren. After sixty-five years I am still with my chosen research."

Ever since she witnessed the total solar eclipse of 1925, Helen Sawyer Hogg has been fascinated by the stars and planets. She received a Ph.D. in 1931 and moved that same year to Victoria, British Columbia, where she began observing star clusters with what was then the world's second largest telescope. Her next move was to Toronto, where she became a professor at the University of Toronto and an astronomy columnist for the *Toronto Star*. *The Stars Belong to Everyone*, her popular science book, brought her much admiration and attention. She is the recipient of many honorary degrees and awards, including having Asteroid 2917 renamed Sawyer Hogg. The Observatory at the National Museum of Science and Technology in Ottawa is also named in her honour.

Margo Timmins

Singer

"After we recorded The Trinity Session, *I had the feeling that if I never created anything again, at least I would have made one thing of beauty. But as fate would have it, the success of* The Trinity Session *has allowed me to find love, to make other records, to be a part of a musical and artistic community I once only revered from a distance, and, most of all, to sing. Singing allows me, in special, rare moments, to achieve a state of almost perfect peace and contentment. It is my hope that through my performances I can communicate something of this feeling to others."*

Margo Timmins had never sung professionally until 1985, when her brother Michael asked her to step into his garage to try singing some songs he and long-time family friend Alan Anton had been working on for their new band, *Cowboy Junkies*. Somewhat nervous and shy of singing in front of her brother, she whispered out her lines. The style stuck and so was born what *Rolling Stone* magazine recently called "the cool miracle of Margo Timmins' voice." With four record releases and over two million record sales to their credit since that fateful day, *Cowboy Junkies* have developed into one of the most unusual and distinctive musical groups in the world. Margo Timmins has received impressive accolades in the press: *Maclean's* included her in their Year-End Honour Roll, and *Esquire* included her in their list of nine outstanding women, saying, "If Marlene Dietrich wore blue jeans, this is how she'd sound." Margo Timmins lives in Toronto with her husband and two Shetland sheepdogs.

P.K. Page

Writer and Artist

"What led me to continue writing poetry after adolescence was some pattern of words that formed intermittently in my idle head, and a dream of saying what I had to say with exactitude and truthfulness. As to what led me to stop writing in middle age — temporarily as it turned out — and start painting, I can only ascribe it to the Portuguese language blocking my pattern of English words and the baroque images of Brazil demanding expression."

The poetry, prose, and paintings of P.K. Page have won her international acclaim. She got her start in Montreal in the early 1940s, where she began publishing her work in small magazines. In 1944 she published her first novel and won the prestigious Oscar Blumenthal Award for poetry, marking the start of a lifetime of accomplishment and recognition. She has published numerous books of poetry, children's books, essays, drawings, a musical text, short stories, and art criticism. She has received five honorary doctorates and the Governor General's Literary Award for poetry. Her paintings have been exhibited in one-woman shows in both Canada and Mexico and are in the permanent collections of the National Gallery of Canada and the Art Gallery of Ontario. She has lived in Australia, Brazil, and Mexico, and now resides in Canada.

Marion Quednau

Novelist

"I write in the confidence that fiction, being the articulation of a dream, can address both men and women readers in a way that crosses boundaries and breaks down barriers, without breaking spirits or suppressing imagination."

Marion Quednau's first novel *The Butterfly Chair* won the W.H. Smith Books in Canada First Novel Award in 1987, and was subsequently published in Britain, Australia, and the United States. She is now completing a second novel entitled *Point No Point*. To complement her life-long association with equestrian sport she is also working on a collection of essays entitled *Five Hundred Falling Horses*. Marion has read from her works in London, England and in Sydney, Australia.

Rosemary Brown

Feminist and Politician

"I am passionately committed to Canada, this country of my choice, even while I retain my love and connectedness to Jamaica, the island of my birth and early years. During the past two years, my work as executive director for MATCH International Centre has given me the unique and challenging opportunity to use the skills and experience that I had gained in Canada on behalf of women from countries and cultures similiar to that of my birth. I would tell the young women of Canada to take responsibility for themselves. To exhort them not to look to fathers, husbands, the government, lottery tickets, or whatever to meet their needs, but to establish long-term goals for their lives, and then to pursue those goals with unwavering singlemindedness."

Rosemary Brown's life pursuit has been to improve the rights of women and minorities. She first entered the political arena in 1972, when she was elected to the British Columbia Legislature. In 1975, she placed second in her bid for the leadership of the national New Democratic Party. She is a founding member of the Vancouver Crisis and Suicide Prevention Society; the Vancouver Status of Women's Council; and she was the Council's first ombudswoman. She was also a founding member of the Canadian Women's Foundation and she is vice-chair of the South African Trust Fund. She was a director for the Canadian Research Institute for the Advancement of Women; and she was the executive director and she is now the special ambassador of MATCH International, a development organization that links the needs and the resources of women in the Third World and in Canada in the pursuit of peace, equality, and social justice.

Nancy Greene Raine

Alpine Skier

"Competition is natural and a great force for bringing out peak performances, not just for the winner but for everyone competing. Competition in sports is good training for real life. It is important, however, not to emphasize winning at an early age. Children should have the chance to experience the fun of competing without the pressure of winning. All those who enter a competition and try hard to do their best, are winners. The losers are those who never enter the race."

The year 1968 belonged to Nancy Greene Raine. She was the overall World Cup champion for the second year in a row; she won the Olympic gold medal in the Giant Slalom and the silver medal in the Slalom; and the gold medal for the Fédération Internationale de Ski Combined Championship. She was also named Canada's Athlete of the Year for the second year in a row. She is a six-time Canadian champion and a winner of fourteen World Cup races. Nancy Greene Raine is an Officer of the Order of Canada and was named to the National Sports Hall of Fame.

Rosella Bjornson

Airline Pilot

"When I told my high school counsellor that I wanted to be an airline pilot I was told there were no women airline pilots and that no airline would ever consider hiring a woman pilot. I decided then and there that I was going to be the best qualified pilot around so they could not refuse my application. I believe anything is possible if a person wants it badly enough and is willing to work for it."

Rosella Bjornson was raised on a farm in southern Alberta. Her father had a small airplane and Rosella became fascinated with flying at a very early age. She attained her private pilot's license at the age of seventeen, her commercial license at nineteen, and her air transport rating at twenty-two. In 1973 she was hired by Transair of Winnipeg as a first officer on the F28 — becoming the first female co-pilot flying a jet aircraft for a commercial airline in North America. Transair eventually became part of Canadian Airlines International. In 1980 she was made a first officer on the Boeing 737 and in 1990 she became Canadian Airlines' first female captain. In May 1991, Rosella Bjornson received a National Transportation Award of Achievement for her exceptional contribution, interest, and success in helping to open the door to women in the field of aviation.

The Right Honourable
Jeanne Sauvé

Former Governor General of Canada

"Canada is one of the most open, demo-cratic countries in the world, in contrast to many countries where access to important positions is more restricted. In Canada everything is possible, including access to education and experience, which can lead to high positions and responsibilities. I am first and foremost a Canadian and well aware of the tremendous advantage this gives me on the international scene. Indeed, it is well known that Canada is highly regarded abroad and, in the aftermath of my life devoted to public affairs, this fact is of great significance in promoting the goals of the Jeanne Sauvé Youth Foundation."

After twenty years as a journalist and broadcaster in Montreal, Jeanne Sauvé was elected to the House of Commons in 1972. As a cabinet member she was responsible for a variety of portfolios during her term in office, including Science and Technology, Environment, Communications, and responsibility for French-speaking countries in the department of External Affairs. In 1980, she was unanimously elected as Speaker of the House of Commons. In 1984, she was appointed governor general of Canada. She is now the founder and honorary chairman of the Jeanne Sauvé Youth Foundation.

Louise Ardenne

Achiever

"To be determined is to have wings."

A severe bout of viral encephalitis left Louise Ardenne with very little long-term memory and an inability to remember anything new for more than a couple of hours. Determined to retrain her brain, she enrolled in Mount St. Vincent University and eventually graduated with distinction. She also regained her memory, with the exception of a seven-year gap. Along the way, she found opportunity to give encouragement and support to other women and to the causes supported by the women's movement. Upon her graduation, she founded The Louise Ardenne Scholarship for Women.

29 – April 19, 1990   Seabright, Nova Scotia

Brenda Taylor

Educator and Counsellor

Charlene Taylor

Chartered Accountant

Brenda Taylor is a member of the Heilstuk Nation from Waglisla, British Columbia. She is a Native Indian home/school worker for the Vancouver School Board and has raised funds for many Native Indian education programs. She also initiated the Native Indian Youth Advisory Society and was a founder of the Spirit Song Native Indian Theatre Company in Vancouver.

"I firmly believe that education is the key to success. I have focused my time and energy for the past twenty years on promoting the education of Native Indian students. For it is the youth of our people who will be our future leaders, the ones who will eventually gain for aboriginal people their rightful place as equal partners in Canadian society."

Charlene Taylor is a member of the Heilstuk Nation from Waglisla, British Columbia. She is the first woman of Native Indian ancestry to become a chartered accountant in Canada. She has participated on several role model panels at Native Education Conferences which are directed at Native youth.

"My parents encouraged me to be aware of both my backgrounds, Native Indian and Scottish. Recognition and respect for both cultures has been advantageous when pursuing my goals. One culture is not put ahead of the other and I strive to take the best from both worlds."

Doris Anderson

Author, Editor, and Women's Rights Activist

"One of the questions I am most frequently asked is: Why are you a feminist? The answer is simple. All the women in my family — my grandmother, two aunts, and my mother, through death or desertion, had to support themselves and several small children alone. The stark choice presented to my generation was either marriage and dependency, or a childless career. Both positions seemed to needlessly punish women — and waste the talents of half the population. I resolved to try to find another way. Why do I keep on now? Because there is still so much to be done, how can I stop, and face myself in the morning?"

Doris Anderson is a well-known Canadian journalist, author, and feminist. A native of Calgary, she graduated in arts from the University of Alberta. She was editor of *Chatelaine* magazine for twenty years and changed it from a ''typical'' woman's magazine to a magazine with a strong feminist edge. She served as president of both the National Action Committee on the Status of Women and as president of the Canadian Advisory Council on the Status of Women. Her resignation from the latter sparked the drive to include an entirely new clause on the equality of women in the Canadian Charter of Rights. She is the author of three novels and a retrospective book on the women's movement in Europe and North America, *The Unfinished Revolution*.

Dr. Mary-Wynne Ashford

Physician and Anti-Nuclear War Activist

"As a writer, teacher, doctor, and woman, I felt I had not been given my gifts so that I could stand on a beach and watch the world be destroyed. While I may not leave my children a material estate, I hope that they will know that I was a part of the movement that ended war."

Mary-Wynne Ashford was a high school teacher raising a family and living in Edmonton before she returned to university in 1978. She graduated in medicine from the University of Calgary and now practises in Victoria. She represents North America as vice-president of International Physicians for Prevention of Nuclear War, the organization that won the 1985 Nobel Peace Prize, and was previously president of the Canadian affiliate from 1988-90. She has also written a proposal for the Department of National Defence to develop a new environmental disaster response service.

Doris Shadbolt

Writer

D oris Shadbolt is the author of two successful books on West Coast artist and writer Emily Carr and a third on Bill Reid, eminent Vancouver artist of Haida ancestry. She is best known for her long association with the Canadian art museum world, especially her twenty-five years of curatorial work at the Vancouver Art Gallery. She has served on many Canadian visual arts boards and in 1976 was awarded the Order of Canada. In 1987, with her husband, she founded the Vancouver Institute for the Visual Arts, a foundation for the support of the visual arts in British Columbia.

"When I was young, art for me simply meant painting and drawing as an absorbing and straightforward occupation having a lot to do with the pleasures of exercising craftsmanly skills. But I came in time to discover art as a broader domain of human endeavour, one constantly changing its forms in response to conditions for its production. It became a challenging and rewarding area for thought and study, one forever eluding the rationalistic procedures that would like to absorb it into the world of clocks and computers. And I came to see art as both a product and a revitalizing process uniquely capable of creating psychic and imaginative space for the artist and the responsive beholder. Despite art's increasingly relentless invasion by a market mentality, that vision has been sufficiently compelling to keep me going for the better part of a lifetime."

Claudia Kerckhoff-Van Wijk

Kayak Champion

"It is fun and a challenge to be a female in a predominantly male, risky sport — I enjoyed breaking these barriers. To be good at something is important — it provides the confidence needed to build the base for your whole life. Whitewater kayaking was my confidence builder. I had talent, the courage to push myself into the unknown, and a burning desire to be the best. But dedication to my dream was the reason for my success."

Claudia Kerckhoff-VanWijk was Canadian whitewater kayaking champion from 1975 to 1985. Throughout her athletic career, she consistently finished among the top five in the world. At her peak, she dominated both male and female competitors, holding the Canadian championship for ten years and winning the bronze medal at the World Kayaking Championship in Wales in 1982. Together with her husband, she now owns and operates Madawasaka Kanu Centre, North America's first Kayak and Canoe school.

Daphne Odjig

Artist

"I was not simply born a Canadian, but born an Indian on a Canadian Indian reserve. The reality of being a legal Canadian in addition to being an obvious Indian initially created some confusion in my young mind. However, throughout my entire life the encouragement of my teachers, parents, and grandparents lit a flame that was never extinguished. My legacy will be my paintings."

Pablo Picasso praised her work; so did Chief Wakageshig, on behalf of the Wikwemikong Reserve. One of Canada's most respected artists, Daphne Odjig's work draws upon her Native Indian heritage. Collections of her work hang in galleries across the country, and her paintings have toured internationally. She is a co-founder of Professional Native Indian Artists Inc. and founder of Indian Prints of Canada. She has been the subject of three film documentaries and has received two honorary degrees. She is a Member of the Order of Canada and the Royal Canadian Academy of Art.

Anne Cameron

Writer

"I would like to be remembered as a woman who called a shovel a shovel and not a manufactured implement designed to assist in bucolic cultivation. And I hope my grandchildren remember me as the Grandma who taught them how to play soccer, ride a bike, swim, laugh from the gut, and respect the earth that gave us nourishment for our bodies and our souls."

Anne Cameron was born in Nanaimo, British Columbia in 1938. She decided at age eleven to become a storyteller and writer. Her mother told her that was a nice dream, but if she wanted to be a writer she'd better find herself a good day job so she wouldn't starve. She finished high school, entered psychiatric nursing, lasted six months, and quit. She worked briefly as an operator for B.C. Tel, and quit. She joined the Royal Canadian Air Force as a medical assistant, and quit. Over the years she has held a variety of jobs including swamper on a freight truck unloading the Uchuk ferry on the Tahsis dock. She is also one of Canada's best-known and best-loved feminist writers. She is the author of nineteen books including the award-winning novel *Dreamspeaker*. *Earth witch*, now in its fifth printing, is one of the best-selling books of poetry in Canada.

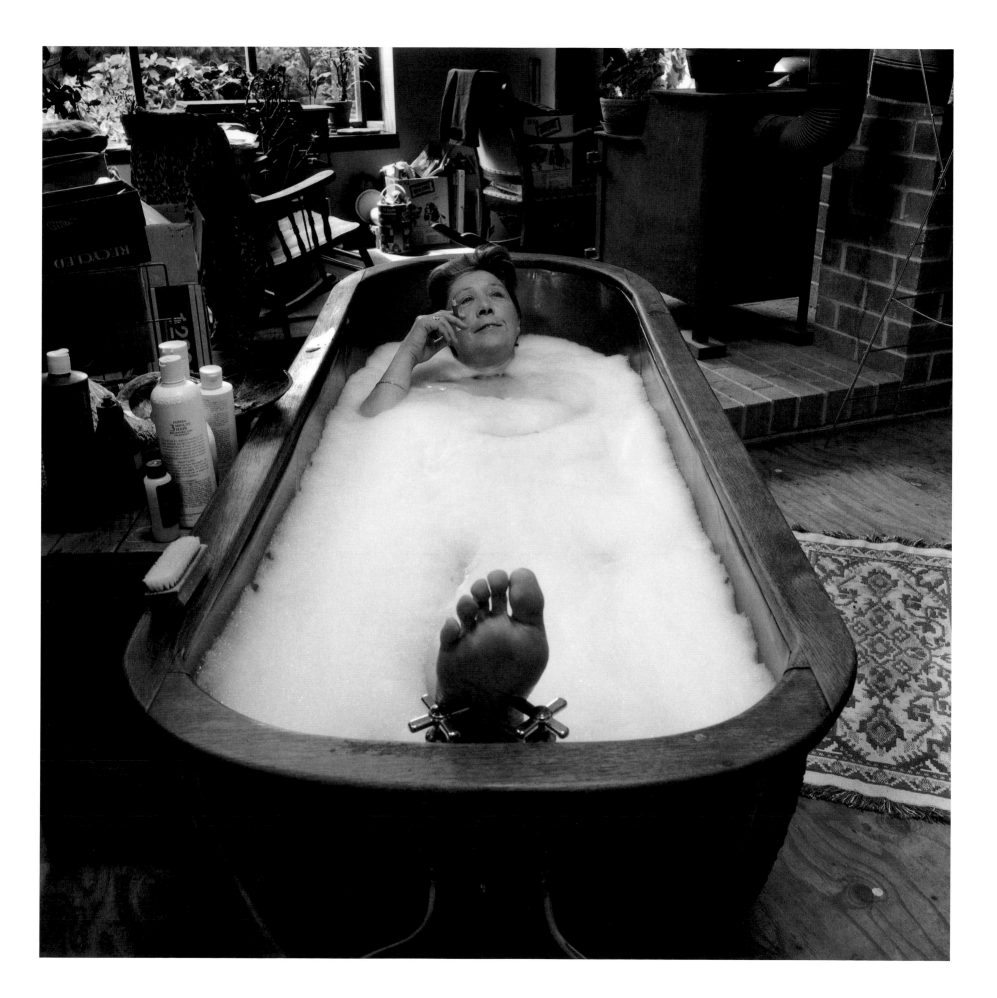

Colonel The Honourable Pauline McGibbon

Former Lieutenant Governor of Ontario

"Being a woman, and, in my career, the first, was a distinct advantage. The disadvantage, if one wants to call it that, was that I had to constantly add to my wardrobe. Unlike a man, a woman can't wear the navy blue suit, tuxedo, white tie, etcetera, over and over again."

Pauline McGibbon was the first woman in both Canada and the Commonwealth to be appointed a lieutenant governor, serving Ontario from 1974 to 1980. She was also the first woman chancellor of the University of Toronto and of the University of Guelph. She is a Companion of the Order of Canada, a Member of the Order of Ontario, and a recipient of thirteen honorary degrees and numerous awards. Her interests range from health and education issues and the arts to the military — she was the first Canadian woman to be appointed as an honorary colonel of a regiment.

Vicki Keith

Marathon Swimmer

"*I am very proud that I am a Canadian,
and I feel that it is important that people
know that. Sometimes I think that we as
Canadians don't believe in ourselves
enough. Canadians are very special people
with a lot to offer. If for any reason I had to
leave Canada, I would continue to proudly
represent my country. Living in Canada
probably helped me develop my skills as a
marathon swimmer — I had the advantage of experiencing all types of weather
and temperatures, so when I jump into the
water I am prepared for anything.*"

Each time Vicki Keith steps out of the water she proves once again that nothing is impossible. The best marathon swimmer the world has ever known, she currently holds over fifteen world records. Vicki Keith is best known for swimming across all five Great Lakes, a distance totalling 275 kilometres. On the final leg of her Great Lakes tour, she broke a world record, travelling 38 kilometres using only the butterfly stroke, the most difficult and tiring of all swimming strokes. She used the same stroke to cross the marathon swimming challenges of the world, including the English Channel, the Catalina Channel, Juan De Fuca Strait, and Lake Ontario. While accomplishing these feats, she has raised close to $800,000 for Variety Club children's projects in Canada and around the world.

The Honourable
Sylvia Fedoruk

Lieutenant Governor of Saskatchewan

"My major goal was always to earn the respect of my peers and I believe I managed to accomplish that. I was able to help pioneer medical physics in Canada — and Canadian medical physicists are world leaders in their research and developments."

Sylvia Fedoruk's life is a long list of impressive accomplishments. She had a distinguished career in medical physics, specializing in the use of radiation in the diagnosis and treatment of cancer and for thirty-five years she was chief medical physicist of the Saskatoon Cancer Clinic. She also served as a consultant in nuclear medicine to the International Atomic Energy Agency in Vienna. She is an avid sportswoman and a member of the Canadian Curling Hall of Fame. In 1986, Sylvia was named an Officer of the Order of Canada and, in 1988, she was appointed lieutenant governor of Saskatchewan.

Buffy Sainte-Marie

Musician and Actress

"I like the idea of being a bridge between Native cultures and the rest of the world. On the one hand, it's a thrill to bring a great concert to a remote reserve; but on the other hand, it's obvious to me that Native people have tremendous contributions to make to world culture — medicine, child-care patterns, lifestyle options, environmental hipness, religion, the arts, government, matricentral philosophies, etcetera. I'd be happy if my music can shine a light on Native life, in order that other cultures can share in the benefits of what we have."

Buffy Sainte-Marie became famous in the sixties for writing intense songs of love and politics, such as "Universal Soldier," "Now that the Buffalo's Gone," and, perhaps her most famous, "Until It's Time for You to Go," which was recorded by over two hundred artists in six languages. She was Billboard's Best New Artist following the release of her first record. In 1976, after the birth of her son and the release of fourteen albums, she quit recording. Over the next five years she appeared on "Sesame Street," and continued to write songs, including "Up Where We Belong," which won her an Academy Award. In 1992, she released her first record in fifteen years.

Dorothy Livesay

Poet

With the encouragement of her parents, Dorothy Livesay had two books of poetry published before she was twenty — *Green Pitcher* and *Signpost*. She is an eloquent feminist and political radical and her poetry has sometimes shocked with its descriptions of sexuality and giving birth. In total, twenty-five volumes of her poetry have been published. She has worked as journalist, social worker, editor, broadcaster, and university professor. Among her many awards she has won the Governor General's Literary Award for poetry twice — in 1944 and in 1947; and, at the age of eighty, she published two books, *The Self-Completing Tree* and a novella entitled *The Husband*.

"There is in the present decade a wild wave of words by younger women in Canada. More and more women are speaking out about their relationship to parents, husbands, and children in exciting experimental prose and poetry. All that we were striving for at the beginning of this century has come to pass."

Marjorie Blackhurst

Senior Executive

"I advise women how to play a full role in organizational life. I also consult with governments on ethics and values. I've become a role model to some and a teacher of M.B.A.s so they can adjust to a strong, mature businesswoman as a leader. I have had, and continue to have, an opportunity to make a difference — making work-places better is what I do. I like what I do — I have a wonderful life."

Marjorie Blackhurst has been a mentor to hundreds of Canadian women executives. With an M.B.A. and a Ph.D. in organizational behaviour, she is well qualified to show corporate leaders how to create and direct strategy, and how to manage and lead their personnel. Her company, CEO Directions, specializes in designing and implementing change programs where deeply held values are involved. She was employed for twenty-five years as a manager, director, and advisor in human resources, public affairs, and corporate strategy for Shell Canada. She serves as senior consulting associate with the Niagara Institute and is on the board of the Metro Toronto YWCA and Scarborough Grace Hospital.

Carolyn Waldo-Baltzer

Synchronized Swimmer

"I've always wanted to be the best I could possibly be. I found a sport I loved, pushed myself to the limit and went as far as I could go — determination got me through twelve years of training. If you have a dream, there really is nothing stopping you except yourself — if you enjoy what you do success will follow."

The 1988 Summer Olympics in Seoul was a special time for Carolyn Waldo-Baltzer. She was the proud flagbearer for the Canadian team, and the first woman to win two Olympic Gold medals for Canada. Her chosen discipline was synchronized swimming and she made Canada a world leader in the sport. In addition to her double triumph in Seoul, she won silver medals at the 1984 Los Angeles Summer Olympics and the 1985 World Final Cup; a duet gold medal at the 1986 Commonwealth Games; and three gold medals at the World Aquatic Championship in Madrid. Carolyn Waldo-Baltzer is a spokesperson for several causes: the RCMP anti-drugs program; the Lupus Foundation; and the United Way. She is also a sports reporter and sports anchor for CJOH Television.

Dr. Geraldine Kenney-Wallace

Scientist

*"Throughout my life I have been intrigued
and motivated by intellectual adventure
and the experiences of travel, both of which
not only fuelled my imagination as a
young girl, but left the permanent imprint
of an arts and science duality in my life.
The social instincts of an artist mix with
the solitary temperament of a writer — the
rigorous thinker and businesswoman
combine with an artistic persona — and I
believe this is not a paradox but a para-
digm. I sometimes feel I am a pioneer sort
of twenty-first century scientist, who lives
in a cerebral time machine and readily
projects from the atomic world of electrons
and nuclei into far away galaxies and
the rings of Pluto."*

Internationally known for her fundamental research in ultrafast laser processes — which occur on timescales of a trillionth of a second or less — Geraldine Kenney-Wallace has studied and researched for over thirty years in the United Kingdom, Europe, the United States, and Canada. Her current position as president and vice-chancellor of McMaster University makes use of the public policy experience she gained as chairman of the Science Council of Canada. Her decade of experience in the public and private sector includes leading negotiations on research and development treaties with Japan. In addition, she is the co-chair of the Foreign Policy Committee of the National Round Table on the Environment and the Economy, a position she has held since 1988.

Dr. Margaret Somerville

Pharmacist, Lawyer, and Ethicist

"Images that permeate my life: bright, strong colours — sun, sand, sky, sea, and birds; the mystery of cats — the sensitivity and receptivity of their whiskers; the sharp wave of joy in breathing the early morning air; the warmth of shared laughter; life as a voyage down a river — moving to discover the unknown in lateral terrain, beauty and wonder, tides, obstacles, dangers and length — an immense adventure; travelling, in hope, with soul-and-mind friends in the world of ideas, imagination, and creativity; and as my father used to say, 'living with the universe'."

Margaret Somerville is the founding director of the McGill Centre for Medicine, Ethics, and Law, a transdisciplinary institute that undertakes research, teaching, and community liaison work on some of the most complex and controversial problems facing society. She is the Gale professor of law in the faculty of law at McGill University and a professor in the faculty of medicine. She is the first woman in Canada to hold a named chair of law. Her work in the university, the community, and the media, and in consulting to governmental and non-governmental organizations, involves her in areas that include AIDS, human rights, reproductive technology, euthanasia, environmental ethics, and allocation of medical resources. She travels frequently, nationally and internationally, to deliver public and academic lectures about these topics on which she also publishes. She has recently been awarded the Order of Australia and elected as a Fellow of the Royal Society of Canada.

Dr. Glenda Simms

Educator

"*Never forget the struggle. It is so easy for women to be neutralized. Young women must never forget their history, because once you forget your history, you no longer know where you are going. I think a lot of Canadian women have not been given a very fair share of the heritage their fore-mothers have passed on to them and the school systems have not done a good job in making them recognize that they have inherited a better world from their mothers. For me, because of the political climate, it feels like I am part of a great revolution — being a woman is very good for me, because it enables me to feel part of this revolution.*"

Glenda Simms has always had a strong commitment to minority, community, and women's issues. A teacher in her native Jamaica, she moved to Canada in 1966. Her first introduction to teaching in this country was in northern Alberta, among the Métis and Cree aboriginal people. She went on to teach Native studies at the University of Lethbridge and at the Saskatchewan Indian Federated College. She has served on numerous boards including a presidency of the Congress of Black Women of Canada. She is currently president of the Canadian Advisory Council on the Status of Women in Ottawa.

May Gutteridge

Humanitarian

"To work full-time in the Church was difficult, as there was no money for parish workers. However, my calling had to be answered."

May Gutteridge is a strong and industrious Anglican parish worker serving the disadvantaged in the centre of Vancouver's roughest neighbourhood. She was the founder and volunteer president of the St. James Social Services Society — an organization she has been part of for thirty years. She now operates a hostel and outreach program with an annual budget of $3 million, but collects no salary for her efforts. May Gutteridge has received many honours for her work, including an honorary doctorate from Simon Fraser University and the Order of Canada.

Leila Joy MacKenzie

Humanitarian

"I believe the vastness and grandeur of Canada to be a celebration of life. Here we enjoy the richness of diversity from every corner of the world. Canada encompasses the best of nature, and embraces the best of humanity. I feel that linked together we have an opportunity to share, encourage, challenge, and inspire, as we join in the spirit of this celebration."

Genuinely altruistic in her efforts and passionate about reaching out to those most vulnerable in society, Leila Joy MacKenzie is a dedicated volunteer and community worker. Her efforts began when she arrived in Toronto in 1964, when she worked for The Canadian Red Cross Society, supervising volunteers and doing administrative work. She is now extremely active in numerous charitable organizations and committees, which include the Canadian Foundation for AIDS Research, the Heart and Stroke Foundation of Ontario, Prime Mentors of Canada, and Women's College Hospital. Her impressive volunteer efforts have been paralleled by an outstanding business career, including the former presidency of Park Med Laboratories, a major medical service company.

Edith Fowke

Folklorist

"Try to find work in a field that interests you even if it means settling for less income than some other field. Working at something you are interested in is enjoyable; work in a field that doesn't really interest you can be soul-destroying no matter how much it pays."

Edith Fowke is an internationally honoured folklorist who has studied, compiled, and shared the tales, songs, games, beliefs, and customs of Canadians. Over the years Edith Fowke has brought together a comprehensive collection of Anglo-Canadian folk songs and children's lore that have been passed on from generation to generation "by oral tradition, either by word of mouth or by custom and practice." She has published over twenty books on folklore and produced almost as many records. Among her most noted books are *Red Rover, Red Rover, The Penguin Book of Canadian Folk Songs*, and *Folklore of Canada*. She is a Member of the Order of Canada, a Fellow of the American Folklore Society and Royal Society of Canada, and founder and editor of the *Canadian Folk Music Journal*. She has been awarded four honorary degrees.

Janet Parsons

Farmer

"In farming we work with mother nature, unpredictable and unforgiving. We deal with sophisticated marketing systems riddled with idiosyncrasies imposed by international forces. We cannot control these two uncertainties. The bottom line then is how we ourselves handle the challenge. My strategy has always been an absolute determination coupled with a daily personal challenge. If I'm better today than yesterday, I've won."

In 1988, Janet Parsons was the first woman to win the W.R. Motherwell award as Canada's Outstanding Young Farmer. The following year she was further recognized for her accomplishments in agriculture with the Canadian Business Magazine Successors Award. Janet Parsons is the co-owner and hands-on manager of Jimanon Farms, a 305-acre dairy farm in northern Ontario. The industry recognizes her as a pioneer in designing an efficient system for the storage and feeding of large round bale forage in dairy herds. Over the years her dairy farm has thrived on her razor-sharp management style. Her business expertise and community leadership skills have gained her both federal and provincial government appointments yet she remains a relatively quiet Canadian who lets her accomplishments speak for themselves.

Evelyn Hart

Prima Ballerina

"I live for dance. I love it, I breathe it, I dedicate my life to it. I want so much to dance beautifully, to be the very best I can be."

The goal of Evelyn Hart's life is to achieve perfection in dance. She joined the Royal Winnipeg Ballet at the age of seventeen and was promoted to principal dancer only six months later. In 1980, she won the coveted Gold Medal and a Certificate of Exceptional Artistic Achievement at the renowned International Ballet Competition in Varna, Bulgaria. Drawing from the pain of personal loss and her often lonely calling, this gifted dancer creates beauty that has captured the hearts of audiences across Canada and on stages worldwide.

Jean Coulthard

Composer

Jean Coulthard first began to attract national attention with her musical compositions in the early 1940s — and as her musical personality revealed itself, she became recognized internationally for the coherent clarity of her music. She taught at the University of British Columbia from 1947 to 1973, and compiled an extensive catalogue of music for students. But it was after she retired from the university that her writing truly blossomed. Today she is best known for her various compositions for piano, her songs, and her chamber sonatas. She has also scored three symphonies, two concertos, two symphonic odes for soloist and orchestra, orchestral suites and tone poems, works for choir and orchestra, and the full length opera, *The Return of the Native*. Jean Coulthard was named Composer of the Year in 1984 by the Performing Rights Organization of Canada, and she is an Officer of the Order of Canada. She has received two honorary doctorates as well — one from the University of British Columbia and the other from Concordia University in Montreal.

"Younger composers are extremely lucky in contemporary Canada. In the early 1930s in the west there were no teachers in my field of music composition. Therefore it was very hard going and I wrote more or less instinctively. After this time I felt that we were the first generation of composers of serious intent; now the situation is completely changed and there are excellent composition courses at all the universities."

Phyllis Lambert

Architect

Phyllis Lambert is an architect of international repute. She is much lauded for her work, which includes the creation of the Seagram Building in New York, the renovation of the Biltmore Hotel in Los Angeles, and the Saidye Bronfman Centre in Montreal. She is also the founder and director of the Canadian Centre for Architecture in Montreal, a museum and study centre with historic and international collections of books, drawings, photographs, and archives that form an unparalleled resource for the study of architecture. A critic and outspoken advocate of urban conservation, Phyllis Lambert is a crusader for restoration over demolition in her role as founding president of the Heritage Montreal Foundation. Appointed adjunct professor in the school of architecture at McGill University in 1986 and associate professor in the faculty of planning at the school of architecture of the Université de Montreal in 1989, she holds twelve honorary doctorates and is the recipient of numerous awards.

"The city is a metaphor for society, for country. It is not monolithic. Our ideas are not hermetic. Our culture is to a large extent global, but if we cannot be meaningful to our local communities we cannot be meaningful outside them. As part of a global world culture the only way to be effective on the broadest basis is to be meaningful to one's local community."

Jean Little

Author

"When I was ten, I began writing stories and poems for my own delight. When I began to write professionally, I wrote about the people who interested me most and for whom I felt the greatest sympathy — children. I set my novels in Canada because it is my homeland. I wanted Canadian kids to discover that heroes and heroines did not have to live in Britain, the United States, or even Prince Edward Island — they could live in places like Guelph. Although I earn my living writing now, I still do it for my own delight."

Jean Little was born to medical missionaries in Taiwan. She was born with severely impaired vision, yet when the family returned to Canada, Jean graduated from the University of Toronto with honours in English literature. She was teaching handicapped children when she decided to try writing. Her first book, *Mine for Keeps*, won the Little, Brown Children's Book Award, and her twentieth book for children is soon to be published. Jean writes with a talking computer and travels with her seeing-eye dog.

Joni Mitchell

Musician and Painter

Joni Mitchell is a unique and well-respected artist. The passion and integrity of her lyrics and music combine with her hauntingly soulful voice to weave a beautiful fabric of song. Joni Mitchell's genius, ever present in her sixteen albums to date, is also apparent in her paintings. Her music, much admired by her peers and many fans, and her stylistically restless paintings, reveal an artist unafraid to express her inner emotions.

"Oh I am a lonely painter

I live in a box of paints

I'm frightened by the devil

And I'm drawn to those ones

That ain't afraid

I remember that time you told me

You said

'Love is touching souls'

Well surely you touched mine

'Cause part of you pours out of me

In these lines from time to time."

"A Case of You"

from the album Blue.

Alice Munro

Writer

Alice Munro writes fiction that speaks to the entire world. Many of her characters and stories are derived from her experiences in small town Ontario and on Vancouver Island, yet the themes of her finely crafted work have an international appeal. She has travelled widely to give readings from her books, to destinations as diverse as Norway, Australia, and China. Her books *Dance of The Happy Shades*, *Who Do You Think You Are?* and *The Progress of Love* have each won the Governor General's Literary Award. *The Progress of Love* was also selected by the *New York Times* as one of the best books of 1986. Alice Munro is a frequent contributor to *The New Yorker* and the *Atlantic Monthly*. Her most recent book, *Friend of My Youth*, is receiving much critical acclaim.

"I think I've had a lucky life. You're lucky when you want to do something as constantly difficult as writing, because you'll never be satisfied and that keeps you going. Then there's the parallel life of the immediate demands on you as a woman that seem at some times to be tearing you apart, but that life too is something I'm glad I've had. It keeps you from getting hollow, and shrinking up inside your own legend."

Juliette

Entertainer

"What I achieved fell in my lap. I was discovered, doors opened, and I never looked back. There was never a set plan in my life. I never dreamed it would be so wonderful."

Juliette Cavazzi made her professional singing debut at the age of twelve in a performance with the Dal Richards orchestra in Vancouver. She first started singing on CBC Radio at the age of fifteen and continued on CBC Television as "Our Pet, Juliette" on Billy O'Connor's "The Late Show." She went on to have her own program, "Juliette," one of the CBC's most popular shows at the time. She spent twenty-two years with CBC Television, always with her own show, and she made three records for RCA. In 1975, she became a Member of the Order of Canada.

The Honourable
Claire L'Heureux-Dubé

Justice of the Supreme Court of Canada

"To be a Canadian is to be given the chance to benefit from this country's tremendous opportunities, to fulfill one's dreams. My dream as a Canadian and a Quebec woman, born in 1927, was to shape my life in accordance with the goal I had set for myself: to work towards a more just world for all. In so pursuing my ideal of justice, I reached two goals: the right to choose my field of endeavour and my entry into the legal profession. Being a pioneer of a kind, with its acknowledged disadvantages, is an exciting challenge that I enjoy to this day. Some talent, hard work, motivation, a positive outlook on life and people, and a bit of luck are a magical combination. It did wonders for me."

Claire L'Heureux-Dubé is a puisne judge of the Supreme Court of Canada. She earned a law degree from Laval University in 1951 and was admitted to the Quebec Bar in 1952. After becoming the head of her law firm in 1969, she was the first woman appointed to the Quebec Superior Court in 1973. She was also the first woman appointed to the Quebec Court of Appeal in 1979. In 1987, she was appointed to the Supreme Court of Canada, again the first woman from Quebec to attain this position. She holds several honorary doctorates from Canadian universities, including her alma mater.

Cynthia Dale

Actress

Cynthia Dale has been in "the business" since the age of five. By the time she was twelve she had done over fifty commercials and many CBC musicals and dramas. Her success is rooted in Canada as a singer, dancer, and actress. Her career highlights include singing the national anthem at a Toronto Blue Jays game, as well as appearing in *Dames at Sea, Heavenly Bodies, Tamara*(in New York City) and *Pal Joey*, for which she won a Dora Mavor Moore Award for Best Actress in a Musical. She was also nominated for a Gemini for Best Actress for her continuing role as Olivia Novak on CBC's "Street Legal."

"Performers must observe what is out there in the world and must also listen to what is inside their soul. We must be prepared to fill ourselves with all that life has to offer — good and bad — and then to reflect it out. To be a mirror to what we have seen and felt and in doing that inspire others to feel themselves. I guess it is this desire to reflect, to affect others, to touch others, that pushes me along, keeps me marching, keeps me performing."

Adrienne Clarkson

Journalist

"I don't think that I could have had the kind of television career I had in any other country but Canada. I think its openness without sentimentality, its opportunities without aggression were exactly the right kind of soil for me to grow in."

Born in Hong Kong of Chinese parents, Adrienne Clarkson came to Canada with her family in 1942 as a refugee. For eighteen years she hosted CBC Television's public affairs programs "Take Thirty," "Adrienne at Large," and "The Fifth Estate." In 1982 she was appointed agent-general for Ontario in France. Upon her return she became president and publisher of McClelland and Stewart and in 1988 became publisher of a McClelland and Stewart imprint — Adrienne Clarkson Books. She is currently producer and host of "Adrienne Clarkson Presents" for CBC Television.

Jane Rule

Writer

"I came to Canada from the United States in 1956 out of the McCarthy era and chose to become a Canadian because Canada seemed to me a smaller, saner, more humane country that welcomed and encouraged young talent. Though the vast majority of books for sale in this country are not by Canadians, we do know our culture is at risk, and we foster as much as we can those young people who are willing to dedicate themselves to the arts. The artist in Canada must still be willing to make great material sacrifices without the promise of conventional success. The only sure reward is the love of the work."

With the publication of the novel *The Desert of the Heart* in 1964, Jane Rule became Canada's first openly lesbian writer. In the dozen books she has so far published, she has shown her concern for a wide range of human experience. In 1978, *The Young in One Another's Arms* was awarded the Canadian Authors Association's Best Novel of the Year. Her books have been widely translated and adapted for radio and film. She has taught at the University of British Columbia and given writing workshops across Canada. She has written for the gay press and been honoured for her work in human rights.

Mary Masales

Farmer

"I was raised on a farm so I guess you just do what you know. I enjoy animals, I enjoy being around them, I enjoy working with them. I've won lots of prizes for my chickens — I like a little bit of competition. Winning shows me my work isn't for nothing. Like this year, chickens from everywhere and mine won. There's a satisfaction in that. A man showed up with a big truck full of chickens, a professional poultryman, goes to all the fairs and competitions. But my chickens won. Raised right here on this little farm, and they got the prize. Made me feel good."

Mary Masales is a widow who raises beef, dairy cows, and chickens, and cultivates an enormous garden. She freezes and cans much of her own food, sells eggs and butter, picks salal and brush, which she sells to a florist, and bakes the best scones and tea biscuits on the West Coast. This year she took her chickens to the fall fair and brought home a suitcase full of ribbons and rosettes, including Reserve Grand Champion. A mother, grandmother, and great-grandmother, she is independent, autonomous, and feisty. In the opinion of many of her neighbours, if there were a few more like her we could replace the senate and get this country back on its feet.

Debbie Brill

High Jumper

"High jumping became my mirror of myself. If it flows out of me then it must reflect what is in me. By looking honestly at all parts of my performance — win or lose — I come to recognize the fears and inhibitions in my life and to find the strengths and understanding to overcome them."

In 1967, when Debbie Brill was fourteen years old, she and fellow jumper Dick Fosbury reinvented the sport of high jumping. Going over the bar backwards enabled her to reach new heights — and it is the technique now used by 98 per cent of the world's high jumpers. In 1969, she was the first woman in North America to jump six feet and she has not only held the Canadian record since that time, but also improved upon it. The Canadian and Commonwealth records now stand at 6 feet, 6–1/4 inches which she set in 1984. She has won gold medals in two Commonwealth Games and a World Cup competition, and has competed in three Olympic Games. In 1980 she was ranked number one in the world but could not compete in the Olympics as Canada boycotted the Games. She set an indoor world record of 6 feet, 6–1/2 inches in 1982 and retired in 1988. She is shown here with her daughter, Katie Rose Coleman.

The Honourable
Kim Campbell

Minister of Justice and Attorney General of Canada

"Being in public life has given me the chance to try to put my vision of democracy into practice; more particularly, to create a society where women don't just aspire to the mainstream but are the mainstream. Virginia Woolf once said, "Anonymous is a woman." I don't want women to be anonymous — I want their voices to be heard. My goal is to see the reality of women's lives become a fundamental assumption on which all public policy is based."

Kim Campbell is the minister of justice and the attorney general of Canada, and the first woman in Canada to hold this portfolio. It is her latest accomplishment in a distinguished career in public service, having served as the chair of the Vancouver School Board and as a member of the British Columbia Legislative Assembly. After election to the House of Commons in 1986, she became minister of state for Indian Affairs and Northern Development. She is currently on the Cabinet Committee for Planning and Priorities and is the senior minister for British Columbia.

Rita MacNeil

Singer and Songwriter

"Being a Canadian makes me feel proud because I believe we have a strong identity living in this country with its landscape and its people. Anyone in the industry here knows it is difficult because people look to the United States to measure success. However, there are changes slowly taking place and the talent here is being recognized. The only advice I can give others is 'don't give up on your dreams,' and those very words and my passion for music have helped me in my achievements so far."

Rita MacNeil is a singer songwriter who hails from Big Pond, Nova Scotia. Although her music celebrates life in the Maritimes, its popularity goes around the world. However, she keeps herself well grounded — performing in her bare feet lets her feel the musical vibrations through the floor — and her loyalty to her roots has won her an audience of fiercely devoted fans. *Flying on Your Own* and *Reason to Believe*, her two hit albums, have both gone platinum, and she has been awarded a Juno to honour her accomplishments.

Sharon Wood

Mountaineer

"I thrive on the potential power of team experience, a shared vision that creates an opportunity for people to aid each other in the discovery of their strengths, the stretching of their self-imposed limitations, and the realization of their dreams. I believe when we do this we are at our best."

Sharon Wood has been to the top of the world and back. On Tuesday, May 20, 1986, Sharon was the first North American woman to reach the 29,028-foot summit of Mount Everest, the highest mountain on earth. To prepare for the ultimate physical, mental, and spiritual challenge, this resident of Canmore, Alberta, also conquered the highest peaks in North and South America. Two climbs in Peru were solo conquests reaching summits of 19,900 feet and 20,350 feet. Sharon is now a popular keynote speaker, inspiring audiences throughout Canada and the United States.

In Memory of
Rosemarie Sanderson-Kirby

Rosemarie took a special interest in this project from its onset. A very successful entrepreneur and businesswoman, she, in the latter part of her career, became executive vice-president of Mainstream Access Corporation, a national career consulting firm.

Although Rosemarie passed away just two months before the project's first exhibition, her company carried on to become a major sponsor of the project and displayed the photographs in Mainstream offices all across Canada.

This book was typeset by Colborne, Cox & Burns of Toronto, Ontario, using a particular cut of Bodoni that originates from the Bauer typefoundry. This Bodoni font is a modified version of Giambattista Bodoni's (1740–1813) original masterpiece.

All photographs were reproduced as 175-line screen duotones at Hemlock ColourScan on a high resolution Dainippon Screen colour scanner. The book was reproduced at Hemlock Printers Limited in Burnaby, British Columbia, on a Heidelberg four colour 40-inch Speedmaster Press, using black and a special mix of brown inks. The paper stock is a 100 lb Sterling Satin Text. Due to the generosity of Hemlock Printers, all images received an in-line spot gloss varnish. The case binding was done by North West Book Company in Surrey, British Columbia.